Janice —
Best wishes.
Judy S. Walter

Simple

Book

Marketing

Judy S. Walter

Layout and design by

Penny Maxson

Printed in the USA

Copyright 2014 by Judy S. Walter

All rights reserved

ISBN 978-1517072612

Partial List of Books

By Judy S. Walter

Sammy, The Talking Cat

The Grey and White Stranger

Nightmare In Europe

Memories of a High School Teacher

Winning the Cancer Battle

Real Food for Real People

Life With Mitzi

Protect Your Health

Table of Contents

Chapter 1 - Introduction   7

Chapter 2 - Online Presence   11

Chapter 3 - Marketing Tools   15

Chapter 4 - Book Launch Party 25

Chapter 5 - How To Dress   33

Chapter 6 - Book Marketing

              Opportunities   37

Chapter 7 - Consignment   45

Chapter 8 - Book Signings   49

Chapter 9 - Shows   69

About the Author   81

Chapter 1

Introduction

You've spent days, weeks, months, perhaps years pouring out your heart and soul into your writing. The task is complete. The book is published. Now what do you do?

Many books have been written on the subject. You can get good ideas from all of them. Many combine the subjects of publishing and marketing. I will not do that.

Some marketing books deal specifically with online marketing. Countless authors have achieved success through online marketing. Then there are ebooks and their promotion. I will save that topic for those who have expertise in that field.

Simple Book Marketing is written for the author who has books in hand and wants to sell them. Let the journey begin.

They have arrived. You take your first book out of the box. You look at it with a smile on your face – hopefully. There it is – your name in print at last. You hold it - admire it – and you are pleased with yourself. You are now an author.

That plus a dollar will buy you a soda – maybe. Now the real work begins. It's time to roll up your sleeves and get to work. You now have the job of selling yourself and your book.

What do I mean? After all, you are a writer, maybe a bit introverted. Sorry. Unless you plan to sit and stare at a box or boxes of books for the rest of your life, you will have to learn to talk to people about your book – why you wrote it and how it can benefit others.

It is not an easy task. Maybe you have time constraints because you work a full time job. Do you work with people? Talk to them about your book. Show it to them. Be proud of your accomplishment. In this business you have to self-promote.

If you have published through a traditional publisher who invests into book promotion, you are fortunate. Not all publishers do. If you are an indie author, I highly recommend you follow some of the suggestions in this book.

Chapter 2

Online Presence

As an author, you should definitely have an online presence. If you published through one of the many self-publishing companies, your package probably included the availability of your book through amazon.com and other bookstore web sites.

If you totally went the independent route, unless you used createspace.com or a similar website, you still want to check into getting your book on amazon.com. You may not make a fortune there, but you still should do it. If you are your own publisher, look into setting up a publisher account with Lightning Source.com and have them submit your book into world wide distribution channels.

The next thing you as an author should have is a facebook page. Don't argue about it; just do it. People love to follow authors on facebook. It is simple. If I can do it, so can you.

The third online presence you should have is a website. You will need a domain name (www.judywalter.com). You will also need a host. Unless you are able to design and maintain your own website, I suggest you get someone to do it for you. Don't spend an outrageous amount on this, however. Look at some online hosts, such as yahoo.com, ipage, godaddy.com, network solutions, wordpress. com. If these don't help you, get a professional.

An online presence lends credibility to you as an author. There will always be those who will buy your book from an online bookstore, such as amazon.com. You don't want to lose those sales.

Chapter 3

Marketing Tools

In preparation for book signings and displays in shows, you should invest in a few eye catching items. None of them is expensive.

First, you will need a simple, plain table cloth that will fit an eight foot table. It can easily be folded to accommodate a six foot, five foot, or four foot table, depending on what you are given at various events.

I personally recommend a solid color that allows your book the best visibility. Print table covers often detract from the book or compete with it for visibility.

The next thing I recommend having made is a mounted display poster of the front cover of your book. An 11"x17" poster is a good table top size. Have it mounted on white or black foam board. For protection, you can have it laminated or shrink wrapped. You can have this made at a local print shop or camera store.

Take it with you to every signing or show. It will fit nicely on a small table top easel. The ones for framed photos work well for this, and they are inexpensive.

The next marketing tool you should have made is bookmarks. You have lots and lots of choices here, so let me make a recommendation. Gotprint.com makes very professional bookmarks for a fraction of what other printers charge. If you are able to design your own to their specifications, do so. Otherwise, get someone else to do it.

You have a choice between one sided or two sided bookmarks. Here are some suggestions as to what to put on the bookmark. You definitely want a picture of the front cover and a brief description of the book. The ISBN number and price should be on it. Some people list amazon.com and other websites where it can be purchased. You may want to list the publisher.

Another option is to put the author's photo on the bookmark. This can go at the bottom on a one sided bookmark or on the back with a short biography of the author if you order two sided bookmarks.

Choose a color that blends nicely with the book cover. Black print is easily readable – unless the book is black. You want to order 14 pt laminated. Order at least 1,000 so that you can give them out everywhere. Always put one in each book you sell.

Finally, design a flier or have someone do it for you. Put your photo, a picture of the book, the date, time, and location of your book signing or speaking event. You can also put one or two comments about the book on the flier.

Run off (in color) five or ten fliers and put them in restaurants, store windows, bulletin boards in the area in which you will be appearing. If the event is in a store or library in another town, mail several to the person hosting the event. Do this for EVERY event or book signing that you do – until you become a nationally known author.

BOOK SIGNING
JUDY S. WALTER

Judy will be signing
Sammy, The Talking Cat

Friday December 20, 2013
1 PM - 4 PM
Tuscarora Mt. Winery
21 E. Baltimore St.
Greencastle, PA

Also featured will be her
amusing cat book
The Grey and White Stranger
and her Holocaust book
Nightmare in Europe

*Enjoy the antics of Sammy
as he keeps the
household on its feet.*

Press Release

Announce the release of your book. Don't expect USA Today to run it, but you must let people know you have just published a book.

If you personally know a reporter, call him or her and ask if he or she will interview you. Otherwise, type an article announcing that you have published a book. Give the name of the book, a short paragraph about it, where it can be purchased, and brief information about you, the author. Include a recent photo of you, and email it to all the local newspapers in your area.

You will get one of three results. Some papers will ignore you and print nothing. Some papers will print the press release. An occasional paper will have a reporter contact you for an interview.

Do this every time you publish a book.

Chapter 4

Book Launch Party

Let the show begin. It's party time. There are several ways a book launch can be done. The choice of venue is entirely up to you – and your budget. You can hold it at a restaurant, wine shop, social hall, church social hall, a pub, a friend's house, or your house.

If you have a big budget (many do not), you can hold it at a nice restaurant. Let's back up and assume you have a more limited budget. In this chapter we will discuss holding a book launch party in your home. Have it clean and presentable. Cat litter boxes and dirty diapers should not be visible.

If you have a friend or relative who is a professional caterer, you may want to elicit their services. Or you and your spouse or a friend could put the whole thing together yourselves.

Choose a date and time. THINK. If everyone you plan to invite works, don't make it 2:00 on Wednesday afternoon. Weekends can be tricky. How about 6PM on Thursday evening? I don't know. Just put a lot of thought into it.

You can make it a wine and cheese party to celebrate the publication of your book (include title). Remember to use the words party, celebrate and publication of your book in the invitation.

Speaking of invitations, you can design postcard invitations at gotprint.com, vistaprint.com, or at your local printer or Staples store. Address them and include your name and return address.

Think of EVERYONE you know within driving distance and invite them. If you invite 100 people, probably 40 or 50 will attend.

If you are putting the party together yourself, here are some suggestions. You can save time (and spend more money) by getting prepared cheese and bologna trays at the deli in your local grocery, or buy the cheese and bologna and cube it yourself.

You can also have a tray with two or three kinds of crackers. A tray with fresh broccoli, carrots, cauliflower and dip is a good idea. Put meatballs in sauce or gravy in the crock pot to heat and keep warm.

A tray with two or three kinds of cookies should also go on the table. You may want a tray with seedless grapes and apple slices or melon to round things out. Because of severe peanut allergies in some people, I would avoid having them. Some people cannot breathe them without risking their life.

You have said wine and cheese (although you can just say party), so have a few bottles of wine, preferably from a local vintner if possible. Some people like sweet red wine while others prefer a white dry wine.

Not everyone will drink wine. Have regular and diet Coke, Ginger Ale and another soda. Freshly brewed, unsweetened iced tea is also a good choice. Provide sugar and Stevia for people to sweeten it.

Very small sandwiches made with a selection of tuna salad, beef salad, chicken salad, or ham salad are also good choices. Remember, this will be dinner for most of your guests if you go with an evening time. These are just some suggestions. You may have other food ideas.

The advertised time is 6:00. When the majority of your guests have arrived, get their attention. It's time for your brief speech. Keep it to five minutes. Be sure to hold up a copy of your book and say something about it – with enthusiasm. Offer your guests signed copies tonight at a discount. If your book retails for $12.95, sell it tonight for $10.00.

Make it easy. Have them on a table with the poster of your book. Have enough books on hand in case everyone wants to buy one. NO pressure. It's a party – a celebration.

Call the clean up crew in the morning.

*This is a sample of an invitation
for your Book Launch party.*

Join the party at my house!

You are invited to a wine and cheese party
at 6PM on Thursday, November 14, 2013
to celebrate the publication of my book.
A variety of cheeses, wines, foods,
and sodas will be furnished,
so bring an appetite - and a guest.

RSVP - 717-261-XXXX
Come and celebrate! *Judy S. Walter*

Now that the big event – book launch party – is over, it's time to get to work on the nitty gritty book marketing. You are a new author, and the task is pretty much all yours.

Maybe you sold lots of books at your book launch, or maybe you sold two or three. It varies from author to author. Do not expect success to fall in your lap. You have to work for it.

If you want to read a collection of success stories in order to stay motivated, I would recommend two books to you: John Kremer's Self-Publishing Hall of Fame and Book Marketing from A–Z by Francine Silverman.

Now we will tackle a list of places where you can promote your book. Not all of them will work for you. The subject matter of your book will also dictate what places are marketing options for you.

Chapter 5

How To Dress

There are those who say we should always wear dress attire to a book signing or event. We no longer live in such a formal society. Common sense should always rule the day.

If you are speaking before a group, dress accordingly. If it is a formal group where those in attendance will be dressed up, you should also. If it is less formal, your attire should be less formal.

I have seen pictures of authors sitting at a book signing table wearing a plaid shirt (unbuttoned) with a t-shirt hanging out over his rotund belly. The same author also was wearing a cap. In my opinion, he was poorly dressed and did not make a good appearance.

Men and women alike should be neat, clean, and well groomed when facing the public. Don't go for the bum look. Take pride in your appearance. The author of *Maddie's Magic Markers* successfully dresses down, but until you reach his level of fame, don't try to imitate him.

A dress shirt, nice blouse, sweater or vest, even a decent looking sweatshirt are all acceptable in certain venues. Nice slacks or jeans (not in holes) can also work. Don't wear a suit if you are selling at a flea market. Remember: be appropriate for the venue.

Chapter 6

Book Marketing Opportunities

Book marketing opportunities are every-where. You just have to take advantage of them. Never be afraid to bring the subject of your book into the conversation wherever you are.

For example, last evening I was attending a Christmas party at a friend's house. At some point the fact that I am an author came up. I was asked about what I write. This is where having bookmarks in my purse comes in handy. I pulled out a couple and handed them out.

One of my books was of particular interest to a couple of people there. One lady and I discussed the book at length. Another lady joined in the conversation. When she found out where I was holding a book signing the next day, she said she was having lunch nearby and would stop in to purchase a copy. She also said her book club might be inter-ested in my book.

Bookmarks are an excellent marketing tool. Yes, I also carry some business cards, but I primarily give out bookmarks. I also leave them with a tip in every restaurant where I eat. I have made friends all over the country by doing this. Sometimes the waitress comes after me and thanks me or tells me her daughter loves cats (if I have left a cat bookmark).

You never know what results leaving bookmarks will produce. Don't underestimate this inexpensive marketing tool.

Book Signings and Speaking Events

Book Signing in Shippensburg, PA

Book Signing in Richmond, VA

Speaking at Smithsburg Library

Sammy Presentation
at Fulton County Library

Speaking at
The Holocaust Memorial Service
in Chambersburg, PA

Signing and selling books
after the Holocaust program

Giving a Holocaust Presentation
at Spring Mills High School
in West Virginia

Chapter 7

Consignment

Some authors like to do this, and some don't. If you service the locations on a monthly basis, it is like having a sales route. If that is not your cup of tea, don't do it. If you can get the shop owner to mail you a monthly check, that cuts down on using your gas.

I have done consignment with some degree of success. At one point, I had twelve locations. Because of my scent allergies, I had to have my associate make the in person calls. As locations stopped selling, we discontinued them.

At one point we were down to four locations. The owner of our most productive location decided to discontinue my books. I have to say that was a real disappointment.

Where can you put your books on consignment? You have to look for independently owned shops or stores. Local pharmacies and gift shops are good places. All you can do is ask. Go to every locally owned store in your area. The places that will carry your book will want a percentage of each sale. Decide what you can live with before you go in. Some places will buy your book outright. Expect to give them a 40% discount.

Keep a record of books placed. A notebook works well for this. Take it with you when you go back to check on sales. Also, give the store your phone number IN CASE they sell out and need more books before you return.

If you place books on consignment beyond your local area, check back by phone or email. Have them send you a check for sales. You can mail more books to them.

Chapter 8

Book Signings

Coffee Shops

Are you a coffee drinker? Do you have a favorite coffee shop? Is there seating in the shop? If so, perfect.

Talk to the owner or manager. Show him/her your book. Ask if you could hold a book signing in the shop. Offer to put up fliers advertising the event. Pick a two or three hour time span – with the help of the owner. Show up about fifteen minutes before the advertised time so you can display your books and poster.

Be sure to submit the event to the calendar of events column in your local newspaper. Post it on your website and facebook. Also post a flier in the coffee shop window about five days before the event. Ask other locally owned shops if you can put fliers in their windows.

You probably want to take about twenty books to the event. Have more in your car just in case you need them. Do not be discouraged if you only sell two. That's two more than you would have sold if you had stayed home.

Make sure you buy a cup of coffee, tea, or a soda while you are there. Be sure to thank the owner for allowing you to hold a book signing in his shop. Be positive. You may want to come back. Experiment with different times.

Chain Book Stores

If your book is available through Ingram and if you have gone with a traditional publisher, you may be able to schedule a signing at a Barnes and Noble or other chain bookstore. Again, stick to a two or three hour time frame. If you do Book Warehouse, some may want you there for four hours on Saturday. Go with the flow.

Barnes and Noble may list you on their web site. In any case, you should email the event to the local newspaper. Send a flier to the store. List it on your web site and on facebook. Send postcards to people you know announcing the event. Remember: the major portion of publicity is up to you.

It is also possible that the store may want you to speak or be a part of a panel. Be open to this.

Libraries

Public libraries are a good place to hold a talk and do a book signing. I have had moderate success with this venue. Get to know the librarians in your area. You have a common bond; you both promote books and reading.

If you are doing a talk or presentation, hang around for fifteen minutes to half an hour afterwards to chat with people and hopefully sell some books.

If you are doing a children's program, request that parents be present. They have the money to purchase your book.

Be pleasant. Smile. Be friendly. If they don't buy today, they may buy the next time they see you.

Be sure to send fliers to the librarian to post. Email the event to the local newspaper. Put up fliers in the area if possible. Announce it on facebook and on your web site.

Thank the librarian for having you. Also, give her a handful of your bookmarks. Offer to return at some point in the future.

Wine Stores

Local, independently owned wine stores can be a good venue for a book signing. Check with the owner. Offer to do publicity – good for them and you. You will need to do all the same things you did for other signings. Announce the event on your web site and facebook. Notify the local newspaper. Put up fliers.

If you don't drink wine, often these stores will have gift items to purchase. You could always buy a bottle of wine for a friend.

Limit the signing to two or three hours. Say hello to everyone who walks in. It's just good manners – and good business. Be friendly, but do not distract from their business.

Cheers!

Gift Shops

Check with the ones in your area. Many are willing to host a book signing. This might be a good idea around the holidays. Make sure you present it to the owner as mutually beneficial.

Do all the same publicity you are now accustomed to doing. At this point it should be second nature to you.

The store owner may want a percentage of your sales. Be prepared to accept their terms.

If your signing goes well, the store owner may be willing to carry your book on consignment.

Book Warehouse

This is a chain bookstore. At this writing, I have only held a book signing in one of their stores. It was fairly successful. Actually, I sold more books there than I did in two Borders stores a number of years ago.

The way it works with them is you supply the books. When you sell one, they ring it through their register. I keep track as well. At the end of the event, you and the manager do the paperwork. About one to two months later, you get a check from the home office for sixty percent of your sales. They keep forty percent. They also handle the sales tax.

In some stores, the manager handles the publicity. I still recommend that you send them fliers and notify the newspaper in the area where the store is located.

Book Warehouse is very receptive to indie authors, so I recommend them.

Independent Book Stores

These are locally owned stores. Many carry used books as well as new ones. Some are easy to deal with. Some are not. One store I checked into wanted $50 for me to do a book signing in their store. Another one wanted 45% of my sales.

A store in Harrisburg where I held a signing was very accommodating. They were not going to charge me anything unless I had to run the sale through their credit card processor. Although I sold nothing that day, I felt it was timing and perhaps the book I was promoting. I plan to go back at some point because they treated me well. Held on a different day and time, the signing may have been successful.

Check into independent bookstores. They can be good, and perhaps they will carry your book.

Flea Markets

Although I haven't tried selling any of my books at flea markets, I know others have been successful at this venue. I've thought about it.

If there is one in your area, give it a try. I recommend you discount your book. For example, if the retail price is $12.95, sell your book for $10.

You will need to be there the entire time the market is open, so take someone with you because you'll need bathroom and food breaks. Dress casually. Flea markets are not places to wear formal attire. You may find this venture to be fun.

If you are traveling, you may want to check into a number of flea markets. The best resource for finding them is Clark's Flea Market USA. You can order it online at *www.flyingcoconuts.com*. It is $7 plus $3.50 shipping and handling. If you want to mail a check, email *ILovNaples2@aol.com* for the address.

Have fun!

Antique Shops

This might be a tricky one. It might depend on the subject of your book. History books and books about various antiques would obviously be a good fit here. Regardless of your subject, check with shop owners.

While doing a book signing at a book store in Gettysburg, the owner of a Civil War shop stopped by and invited me to do a signing in her store. You just never know.

Again, point out that you will do some publicity – notify local newspapers, put up fliers, announce it on your web site and facebook. Remind them that the store may get additional traffic because of your book signing.

They may or may not want a percentage of your sales. Be prepared to accept their terms. Who knows? They may want to carry your book.

Restaurants

Although I have never done a signing in a restaurant, I was asked to do one at a local restaurant I frequent. It was to be in conjunction with Santa. I had to decline because I was scheduled somewhere else.

A couple of years ago I read in the Paxton Herald that an author in the Harrisburg area was going to hold a book signing - at breakfast, no less – at a restaurant in that area. So this is something authors do.

Check into it. If there is a local restaurant that you frequent, ask the owner if you can hold a book signing there. Once again, you'll do the publicity. Just don't spill coffee or get food on the books.

Historical Society Events

If your book is about local history, check into speaking at one of the historical society meetings in your area. Afterward, you can sell your book.

I live in a Civil War town. A local author whose book on a Civil War general was recently published, spoke at a historical society meeting and sold books afterward.

All local history events are good opportunities for your history book. Be prepared to speak. Don't give away the contents of your book, however, because then there will be no need for people to buy it.

If there is a celebration of the founding of your town, that is also an opportunity for you to display and sell your book.

If your town has a museum, see if they will sell your book, if appropriate. Often museums will carry the works of local authors.

Cooking Demonstrations

Some communities hold food tasting events or cooking demonstrations. Depending on the venue, you may be allowed to have a table and do a book signing. I would think it would be easy to get in if you have written a cookbook.

If you are a local author and the event is being held in your town, ask. The worst that can happen is for them to say no.

The same thing is true of wine tasting events (other than wine stores). Ask. You'll never know until you ask.

Nutrition Stores

My first book was health based. Several nutrition stores in the area and in surrounding towns carried it on consignment. One store bought six outright. One store carried it at the register until the store was sold. The new owners stuck it in the back room, away from customers. At that point I removed what copies were left.

If your book is health related, check into independently owned nutrition stores. You may be able to get them to carry your book or allow you to do a book signing.

I once did a book signing at a nutrition store in Richmond, VA. They were very accommodating. Afterward, they bought several copies for the store. It was a good experience.

Club Meetings

Do you belong to an organization – Lions Club, Rotary, etc? These clubs are always looking for speakers. Check into speaking at one of their meetings. You should be able to sell your book afterward.

Make sure you list the event on your web site, facebook, and in the local newspaper.

If you can't think of these organizations, do a Google search. Try service organizations in your search. Also, go through your list of friends and relatives to see who might be a member of one of these organizations. They can put you in touch with the program chairman.

Don't be bashful. Speak up. Promote yourself and your book.

Home Parties

This may be a tough one. You have already had your book launch party, so that's done.

Lots of people are involved in home party businesses. If you know someone, check to see if you can tag along and have a table there with your book. Just be sure your book is appropriate for the party.

If it is a toy party and you have written a children's book, it's a perfect match.

If it's a Tupperware party, and you've written a book that appeals to women, that should work. A cookbook would work well here.

Use your imagination. Opportunities are endless.

Nursing Homes

This may seem like a strange place to market, but if the subject of your book is of interest to senior citizens or their grandchildren, look into speaking or putting on a program in a nursing home. I have a friend who has written a series of books on the orphan train movement in the U.S. She speaks and sells books in nursing homes.

Contact the activities director in each nursing home and offer to speak or do a presentation. Some authors charge; some do not. If you are new, I suggest you don't. Just make sure they will allow you to sell your books.

A word of caution – the residents need to be of sound mind for this to work.

Chapter 9

Shows

Book Festivals

These are great events and can be lots of fun. You get to network with other authors and publishers.

Look online for book fairs or festivals that you may want to participate in. A fee is usually required. Often travel expenses are involved. Remember to deduct these expenses on your income tax return.

Because my associate and I have been willing to travel, we have met lots of interesting authors and publishers, including the late Michael Palmer. I've also expanded my readership.

One lady to whom I had given a bookmark drove two hours in the rain to buy two copies of my Holocaust book. Wow!

If you drive or fly a distance to a show and stay in a hotel, think of it as a mini vacation.

Book festivals are fun. Sometimes you make money and sometimes you don't. But they are fun. You always meet new people and reconnect with those you met previously.

If you have your sights set on the Miami Book Festival, the L.A. Times Book Festival, or Book Expo America, you should plan to go in under Combined Book Exhibit or another organization.

Do an internet search to find book festivals.

Health Fairs

In order to exhibit at a health fair, your book must be health related. Check with your local chamber of commerce to see if there are any health fairs in your area. Also, go online to see if you can find any. Check with your local hospital.

Also, sometimes local chiropractors have health seminars. Likewise, check with nutrition stores in your area. Even churches sometimes host health seminars.

Day spas and massage therapy clinics may be another source. Senior centers have been known to host health fairs.

Put your thinking cap on and your investigative skills to work.

Craft Shows

These shows range in size from very small to very large with fees ranging from $10 to several hundred. Start with the small, local craft shows. They are most prevalent in the spring and fall. Look in the local newspaper or shopper to find them. You can also Google craft shows in each state.

When you find a craft show you think you want to do, call or email and ask for an application. Fill it out and return it with your check right away. Shows fill up quickly. Also, ask to be located away from candles and soaps so that your books do not absorb the smell. Some people have allergies and will not be able to buy your book if it smells.

Craft shows can be fun. Arrive about thirty minutes before the show starts so that your display is completely set up when the public starts arriving. Often food will be available to purchase.

Be sure to give out bookmarks to as many people as possible, even if they don't buy. I learned that from two other authors I met at book festivals. They may order online at a later date. I've done that.

Like other shows, you will meet lots of

people. Craft shows can be a successful venue. I've sold as few as three books and as many as twenty-seven at a show.

Remember: your application fee (rent) is tax deductable.

Church Bazaars and other events

You probably know what opportunities exist for you at your church – if you have a home church. Check around your community to see what is available in other churches. Depending on the subject of your book, you may be able to speak to a group.

Let me give you an example. I am friends with an author who has written a faith based book. She has spoken in many churches and sold books afterward. She will be the speaker at the UMW tea this spring at my church.

You may be able to rent a table at a church bazaar. Just set up as you would at a craft show.

State or Regional Fairs

I have never done one of these. Renting a space can be expensive. I know one author on the West Coast who tried this. I don't know how he made out. Maybe you can share a booth with another vendor / author.

If there is a fair in your area, check into the cost. Maybe they have a craft day, and you can set up then.

If this is too costly, don't do it.

You have given birth.
Let all the world know it.

About the Author

A graduate of Shippensburg State College, Judy S. Walter is a retired high school teacher. A multi-genre author, *Simple Book Marketing* is her eleventh book. Walter also promotes an arts and crafts show and a book festival in her hometown. She resides in PA with her cat, Mitzi.

46413573R00047

Made in the USA
Charleston, SC
17 September 2015